# Prehistoric Reptiles

# CONTENTS

© Aladdin Books Ltd

*Designed and produced by*
Aladdin Books Ltd
70 Old Compton Street
London W1

All rights reserved

*Printed in Belgium*

*First published in the
United States in 1984 by*
Gloucester Press
387 Park Avenue South
New York NY 10016

ISBN 0-531-03480-1

Library of Congress
Catalog Card No. 77-10464

*Certain illustrations have previously appeared in the "CloserLook"
series published by Gloucester Press.*

A CLOSER LOOK AT

# Prehistoric Reptiles

## DOUGAL DIXON

Illustrated by
### RICHARD ORR

Consultant
### JOYCE POPE

Gloucester Press
New York · Toronto · 1984

# Animals in the past

There were animals living on earth a long time before there were people. We know this because we can find their bones and other remains in the rocks. These remains have been turned to stone and we call them fossils. Ancient animals were not like the animals today. Sometimes we can find the whole of an animal's skeleton, sometimes even its skin. When we do, we can work out where the muscles were. Then it is easy to see what kind of animal it was. Often we find only a single bone. That makes it difficult to know what the animal looked like.

## How old are the fossils?

The oldest fossils are inside the oldest rocks, so we can see what animals were living at different times in the earth's history. We give long names to the periods when different animals lived. The oldest fossils are from the Precambrian period, more than 570 million years ago. They are of little animals that lived in the sea. No animals lived on land until the Devonian period, 410 million years ago. People did not appear until the Pleistocene period, only about two million years ago.

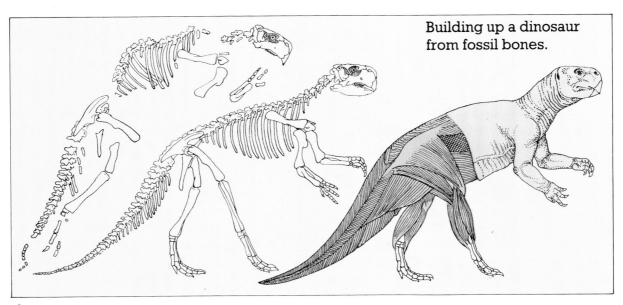

Building up a dinosaur from fossil bones.

The different fossil periods.

*Each number shows
the millions of years
ago that each fossil
period started.

Usually, the older a fossil,
the deeper it is buried in
rocks. Life first began in the
sea. Land animals
appeared in the Devonian
period. The age of the
dinosaurs was between the
Triassic and Cretaceous
periods.

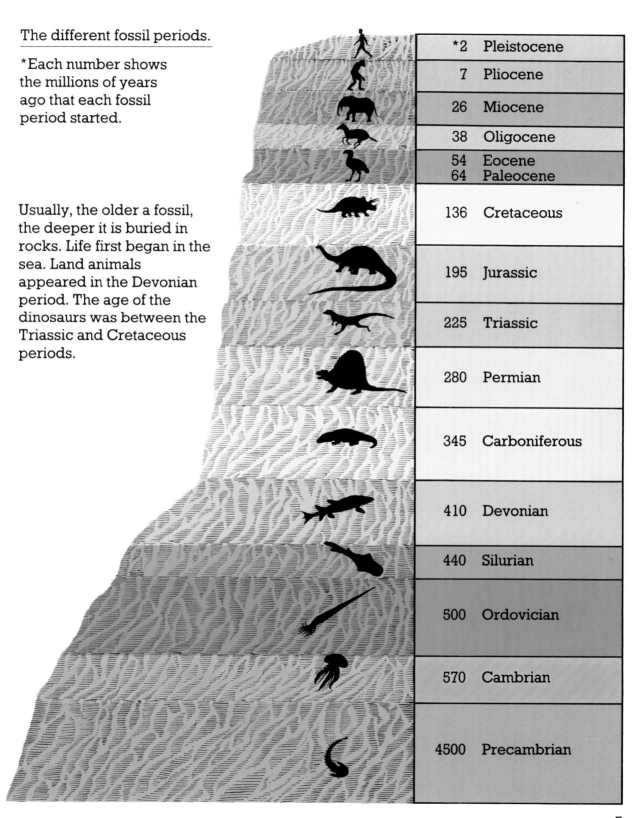

| *2 | Pleistocene |
| 7 | Pliocene |
| 26 | Miocene |
| 38 | Oligocene |
| 54 | Eocene |
| 64 | Paleocene |
| 136 | Cretaceous |
| 195 | Jurassic |
| 225 | Triassic |
| 280 | Permian |
| 345 | Carboniferous |
| 410 | Devonian |
| 440 | Silurian |
| 500 | Ordovician |
| 570 | Cambrian |
| 4500 | Precambrian |

# What is a reptile?

Have you ever seen snakes slithering along, or a lizard scampering up a tree, crocodiles lying at the side of a river or tortoises hiding in their heavy shells? Even if you have not seen them in the wild, you have probably seen them in zoos, in books, or on television. These animals are called reptiles. Reptiles were the first main animals on land. After them came the mammals, and most of the big animals we see today are mammals. Reptiles are quite different from mammals. They lay eggs, and they have scaly skins instead of fur. Their bodies grow cold in cold weather and hot in hot weather. Mammals give birth to live young, and they can keep their bodies the same temperature all the year round.

### Where do reptiles live?

Nowadays reptiles mostly live in hot countries. They cannot stand the cold winters in cooler countries. The only reptiles found in cold countries are small lizards and snakes. In winter, they hide underground to keep warm. Once, it was much warmer everywhere on earth, and big reptiles lived all over the world.

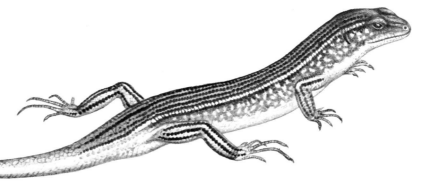

Like all reptiles, lizards and crocodiles lay eggs. The egg has a shell that protects the baby animal. The baby feeds on the yolk until it hatches.

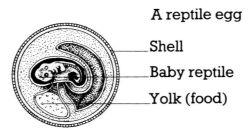

A reptile egg

Shell

Baby reptile

Yolk (food)

A baby crocodile with its parent.

# The first reptiles

The first reptiles lived in Carboniferous times, about 300 million years ago. At that time the only other large land animals were the amphibians. The amphibians were like today's frogs and newts. They had to spend much of their lives in the water. They laid eggs in the water and these hatched into tadpoles. The first reptiles were much better at living on land than the amphibians. Because reptiles' eggs were covered with a shell, they could be laid on land and not dry out.

## The world of the first reptiles

The reptile in the front of the picture, called Hylonomous, lived in a swampy forest. The trees of this forest were quite different from today's trees. There were giant types of ferns, horsetails, and clubmosses. Nowadays these plants are much smaller. Insects like cockroaches and giant dragonflies lived here, and Hylonomous probably chased and ate them. When these forests died, they were slowly covered over with layers of mud and sand. Nowadays all this buried wood has turned to coal, just as the buried bones have turned to stone.

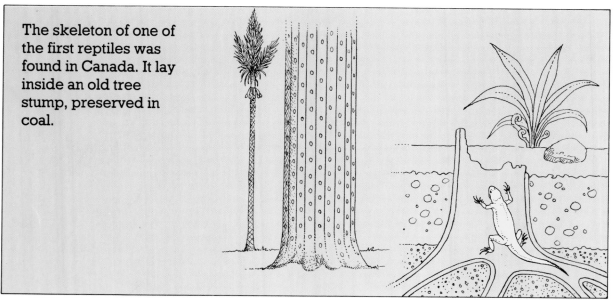

The skeleton of one of the first reptiles was found in Canada. It lay inside an old tree stump, preserved in coal.

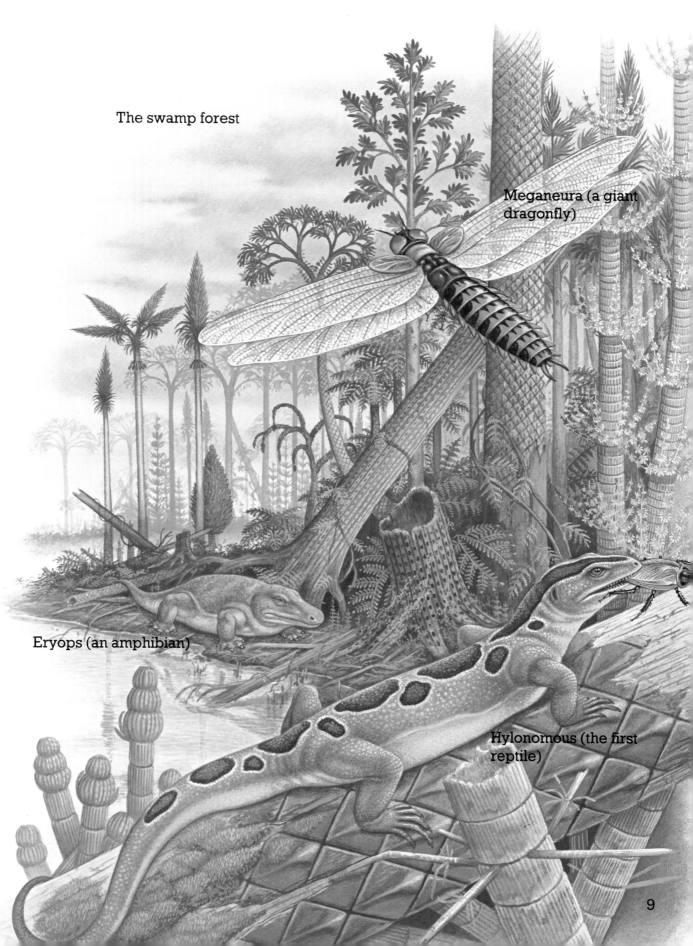

The swamp forest

Meganeura (a giant dragonfly)

Eryops (an amphibian)

Hylonomous (the first reptile)

9

# The move to land

When the reptiles lived in swampy forests, they were never far from water. But the swamps dried up and the forests died. The reptiles had to live in much drier climates, and slowly their habits and their appearance changed. All sorts of new reptiles lived in the Permian period, 280 million years ago.

The most interesting of these new reptiles looked like mammals in some ways. They were covered with fur, and their teeth were like mammals' teeth. They even took care of their young after they hatched, just as a mammal looks after its young after they are born. Eventually, their descendants became mammals, but in Permian times they were still reptiles.

These mammal-like reptiles looked a little like modern mammals – the fierce, meat-eating wolf and the water-loving hippopotamus.

Lystrosaurus

## Killer reptiles

The earliest reptiles fed on the amphibians and insects. They were quite small, so that they could chase their food quickly. Later, some of them ate plants. They became much larger. They did not need to run fast, because their food grew all around them. After a while, some of the meat-eaters became much larger too. Then they could kill and eat the big plant-eaters. These killer reptiles had strong teeth like those of a dog. With these teeth, they chewed tough meat. One of the mammal-like reptiles was called Cynognathus. Its name means "dog mouth." Some plant-eating reptiles, such as Lystrosaurus, took to the water to get away from them.

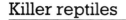

Cynognathus

# Reptiles by the sea

While the mammal-like reptiles were living on dry land during the Permian period, other types of reptiles were living by the sea. By Triassic times, 225 million years ago, the seaside reptiles had changed into all sorts of different types. Macrocnemus looked like one of today's lizards. Tanystropheus had a fantastic neck, 3 m (10 ft) long, which was probably useful for fishing. Askeptosaurus had a very long tail. It could swim like a sea serpent and chase fish. There were even reptiles that flew, such as Eudimorphodon.

## The inland sea

The skeletons of all these animals were found in Poland. In Triassic times there was a huge inland sea there. The animals lived in caves in the cliffs along the shore. There is no sea in Poland now. Changes like this have happened everywhere. It is not just the animals and plants that were different millions of years ago. The landscapes, too, looked quite different from those that we know today.

Tanystropheus

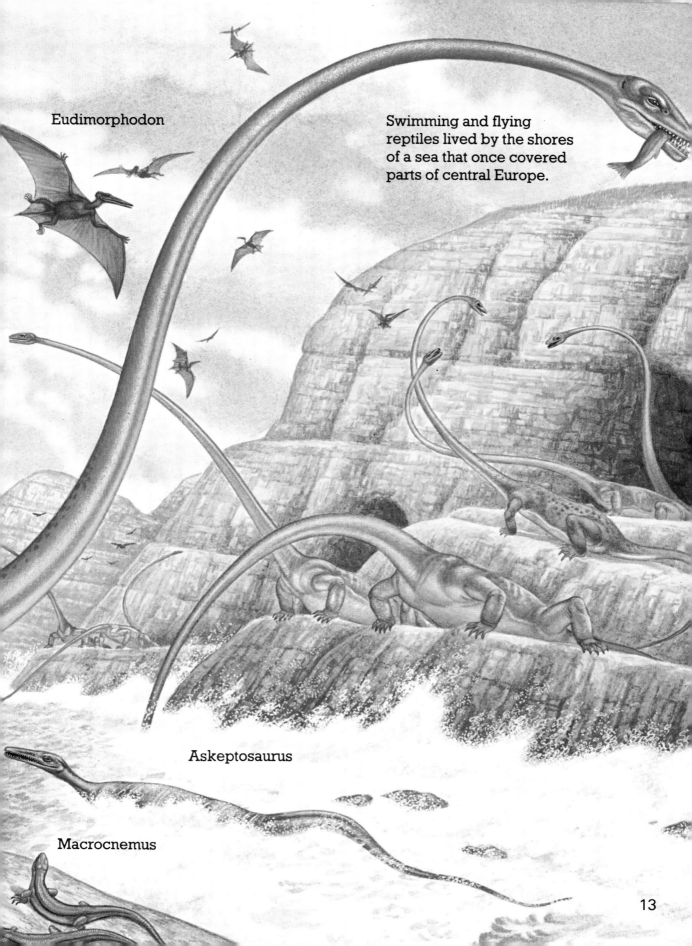

Eudimorphodon

Swimming and flying
reptiles lived by the shores
of a sea that once covered
parts of central Europe.

Askeptosaurus

Macrocnemus

13

In the early Permian period, mammal-like reptiles (dark green) looked like big lizards. Archosaurs (light green) looked like small lizards.

Later in the Permian period, the mammal-like reptiles began to look more and more like mammals, while the archosaurs looked more and more like crocodiles.

In the Triassic period, some of the mammal-like reptiles became true mammals. The rest vanished. The archosaurs became fully land-living animals.

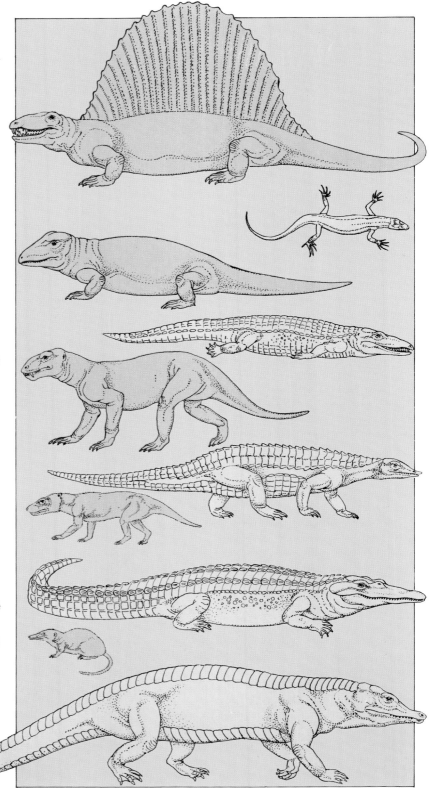

# The terrible lizard

During the Triassic period, the mammal-like reptiles slowly disappeared. Some kinds died out completely. Others became less like reptiles and more like mammals. Their descendants were small, mouselike animals, the first mammals. Now the strongest animals on earth were the reptiles that had stayed near the water, while the mammal-like reptiles ruled the land. These were shaped like crocodiles, and they swam and ate meat – just as crocodiles do today. They were called the archosaurs.

### The new rulers

With no dangerous mammal-like reptiles left on land, the archosaurs came out of the water. They had strong hind legs and a long tail to help them swim. On land they walked on their hind legs, stretching their tails out behind. This was the shape of the first dinosaur – a Greek word meaning "terrible lizard." The dinosaurs ruled for 150 million years. Ornithosuchus was one of the first dinosaurs and looked like a crocodile standing on two legs. Another, Coelophysis, had a small, light body like a bird's.

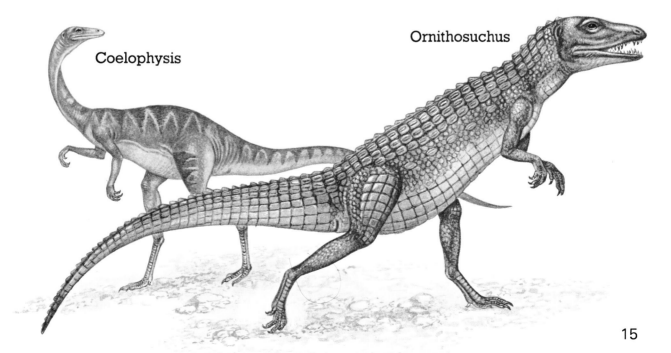

Coelophysis

Ornithosuchus

# Large and small

The dinosaurs soon became the biggest animals ever to walk the earth. In the Jurassic period, 195 million years ago, many dinosaurs became heavy plant-eaters and went back to walking on all fours. Apatosaurus was one of the largest. It reached a length of over 20m (66ft) and weighed 30 tonnes (33 tons). With its long neck it could reach many food plants almost without moving. Compsognathus was one of the smallest dinosaurs living at that time.

Apatosaurus

Compsognathus

16

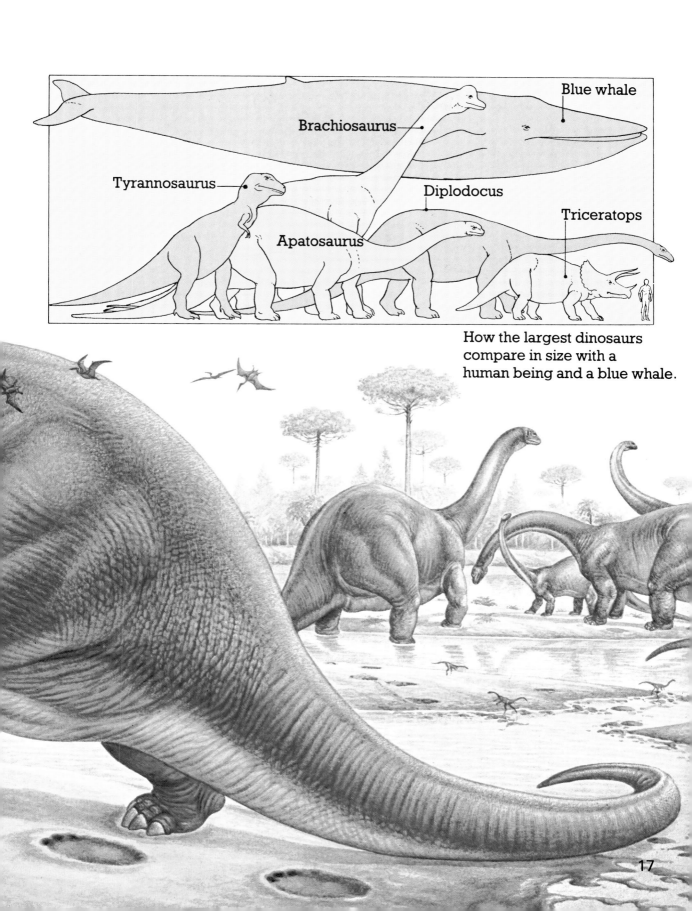

Blue whale

Brachiosaurus

Tyrannosaurus

Diplodocus

Triceratops

Apatosaurus

How the largest dinosaurs
compare in size with a
human being and a blue whale.

17

# Armored giants

Meat-eating dinosaurs also became huge. Allosaurus, for example, measured 11m (36ft) long. Some of the big plant-eaters needed armor to protect themselves from its great teeth and claws. Stegosaurus had bony plates down its back and spikes on its tail. A battle between these two mighty animals must have been a terrible sight.

Stegosaurus

Allosaurus

# Speedy midgets

As we know, not all dinosaurs were huge. Some were quite small and nimble. At the first sign of danger, they could run away swiftly from a clumsy, giant meat-eater. Hypsilophodon ate plants and was only about 2m (7ft) long. Struthiomimus was a little larger – about 3.5 m (11 ft) long. It looked rather like an ostrich, and could run like one too! It raided the nests of other dinosaurs and ate their eggs.

## Small but fierce

Some small meat-eating dinosaurs attacked much larger animals than themselves. Deinonychus was only 3 m (10ft) long, but it was very fierce. It had a vicious, sicklelike claw on its foot. It hunted in packs, and killed large dinosaurs by ripping and slashing at them.

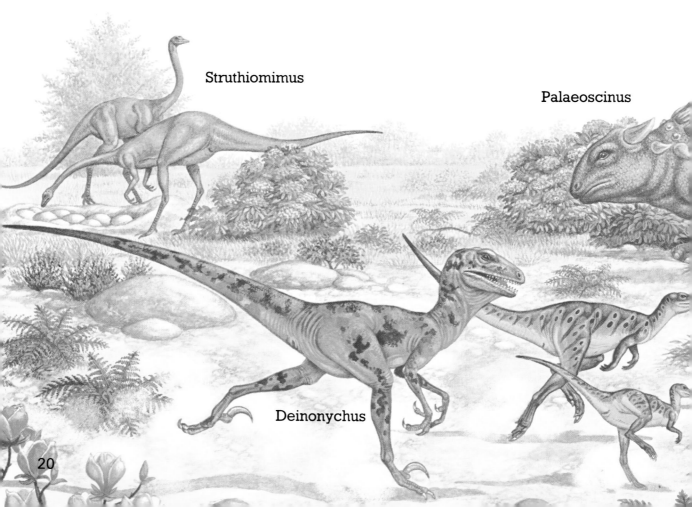

Struthiomimus

Palaeoscinus

Deinonychus

In the Cretaceous period, armored dinosaurs like Palaeoscinus lived side by side with small, fast-moving dinosaurs and also with modern-type birds.

Heron

Hypsilophodon

21

# The last dinosaurs

The end of the Cretaceous period, about 64 million years ago, was also the end of the age of dinosaurs. Some of the last dinosaurs were the most amazing. Triceratops was about 9m (30ft) long. Its head was covered with armor that stretched in a shield over its neck. It had three forward-pointing horns that must have been deadly weapons. It used these to defend itself and its young from the meat-eaters. It may also have fought against other Triceratops to win a mate. It walked on all fours but its front legs were shorter than its hind legs. This shows that, a long time in the past, its ancestors walked on two feet.

Some dinosaurs still walked upright at the very end, Corythosaurus, for instance. This dinosaur had a bill rather like a duck's. With this it could chew tough, waterside plants, as ducks do, so it probably lived near water.

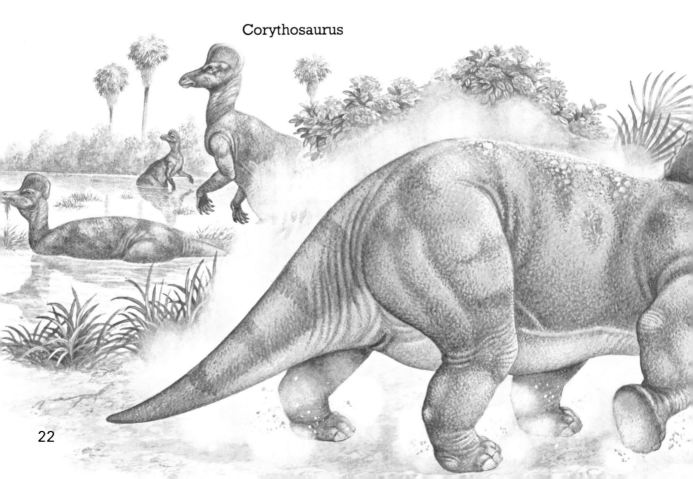

Corythosaurus

### Why did the dinosaurs die out?

We do not know how or why the dinosaurs died out. The climate of the earth had been the same for millions and millions of years. It changed at the end of the Cretaceous period. Perhaps the dinosaurs could not live in this different climate. New plants, like the plants we have today, appeared at the same time. Perhaps the plant-eating dinosaurs could not eat these and starved to death. Then the meat-eaters would have starved, too.

### Death from space?

Some scientists think that a huge meteorite fell from outer space and struck the earth. They say that this made dust clouds that cut out the sunshine for a few years, so plants died and the dinosaurs starved. All we know for sure is that the dinosaurs disappeared.

Triceratops

# Sea serpents

In the Jurassic and Cretaceous periods, there were big reptiles in the sea as well as on land. These sea reptiles had streamlined bodies, and flippers instead of legs. They lived the way sea mammals such as seals, whales, and dolphins live today. Plesiosaurus was rather like a seal, and chased fish. With its small head and long neck, it could also snap at fish swimming around it. Whale-like Liopleurodon ate big squids, just as sperm whales do today. Ichthyosaurus looked like a dolphin. It had long, toothed jaws, a finned tail, and a large fin on its back.

Liopleurodon was about 12m (39ft) long and probably moved quite slowly. Plesiosaurus and Ichthyosaurus were smaller. They chased fish swiftly through the oceans.

Plesiosaurus

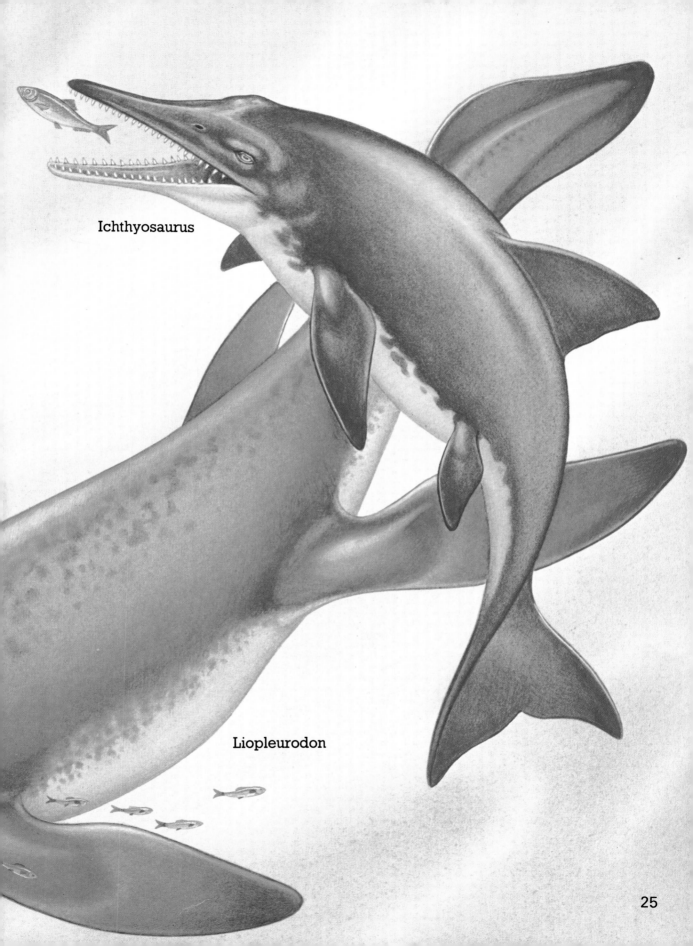

Ichthyosaurus

Liopleurodon

25

# Early flight

Before there were birds, there were reptiles that flew.
These lived in the Triassic, Jurassic, and Cretaceous
periods, at the same time as the dinosaurs. The first ones
glided and did not really fly. Their wings were wide strips
of skin or scales attached to their bodies. They could leap
from a high perch, open these wings like a parachute, and
glide down to the ground. Later, some reptiles had bigger
wings, stretching from their long, strong arms to their
bodies and hind legs. These were the first true fliers. They
were called pterosaurs.

Some pterosaurs were larger than eagles. These had no
teeth and ate fish. Others were as small as sparrows and
ate insects. They were all covered with fur, which helped
to keep their bodies warm.

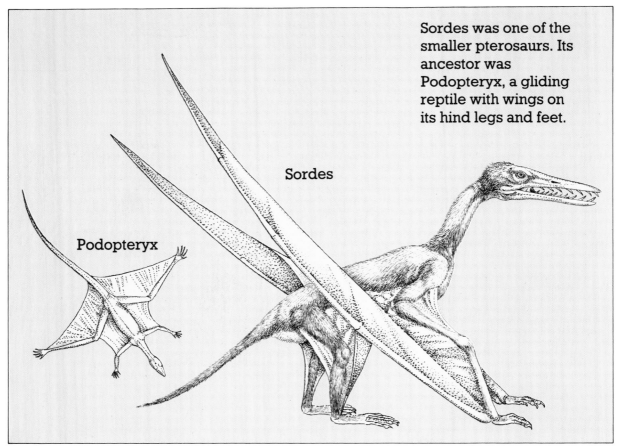

Sordes was one of the
smaller pterosaurs. Its
ancestor was
Podopteryx, a gliding
reptile with wings on
its hind legs and feet.

Sordes

Podopteryx

## The first birds

Birds began to appear in the age of dinosaurs. Archaeopteryx was the first bird. It lived in the Jurassic period. It was descended from a small dinosaur, probably Compsognathus.

The skeleton of Archaeopteryx looked far more like the skeleton of Compsognathus than like the skeleton of a bird. It had a long, bony tail, there were claws on the wings, and it had jaws and teeth instead of a beak. But Archaeopteryx did have feathers covering its body. The long feathers on its arms and tail enabled it to fly.

Archaeopteryx

Compsognathus

27

Quetzalcoatlus

# Flying dragons

The largest flying animal that ever lived appeared at the end of the age of dinosaurs. It was a pterosaur called Quetzalcoatlus. It was as big as a small airplane, with a wing-span of 10 m (32.5 ft). It soared like a glider on currents of air. Its home was the forested plains of North America.

## Reptilian vultures

Quetzalcoatlus glided until it saw a dead animal on the ground. Then it would swoop down with dozens of others and eat the carcass, just as today's vultures do. The biggest of the meat-eating dinosaurs, Tyrannosaurus, was 12m (40ft) long. It was probably too big to chase live animals, and fed on dead ones instead.

Tyrannosaurus

# The survivors

By the end of the Cretaceous period, these strange reptiles had vanished. The last sea reptiles, and the last great reptiles of the air and the land – the pterosaurs and the dinosaurs – all died at around the same time. This happened about 64 million years ago. That was when the mammals took their place.

### The mammals rule

The mammals had appeared at about the same time as the dinosaurs. But when the dinosaurs were the rulers of the earth the mammals stayed very small and unimportant. In a few million years after the death of the big reptiles, the world was filled with cats, monkeys, elephants, horses, whales, and all sorts of other mammals. At last people arrived on the scene.

## Modern reptiles

One odd reptile that is alive today has not changed since the days of the dinosaurs. This is the rare tuatara in New Zealand. Other reptiles we know much better have hardly changed in all that time. Crocodiles look much like their ancestors did 200 million years ago. Tortoises and turtles like those of today lived in the Triassic period.

There are still plenty of birds on the earth. They had the same ancestors as the dinosaurs. A few scientists think that they are so much like them that the birds are really dinosaurs still alive today!

# Glossary

**Amphibian** An animal that lives both in the water and on land. Its young are tadpoles that live in the water.

**Climate** The kind of weather that an area has over a long period of time.

**Clubmoss** A plant related to the ferns. It has a stem, tightly covered with tiny leaves.

**Fossil** The remains of an ancient animal or plant embedded in the rocks.

**Glider** An animal or a machine that flies without any power. Gliding airplanes have no engine. Gliding animals do not flap their wings.

**Mammal** The highest form of animal life. Mammals bear their young alive, can keep their bodies the same temperature in cold or hot weather and usually have fur. We are mammals. So are dogs, elephants, deer, mice, bats, and whales.

**Pterosaur** An extinct flying reptile. It had wings of skin held up by outstretched arms.

**Reptile** An animal that lays eggs on land, is covered with a scaly skin, and whose body temperature changes with the temperature of its surroundings.

**Skeleton** All the bones of an animal, placed together to form the framework to support the animal.

# Index

PRINTED IN BELGIUM BY

proost
INTERNATIONAL BOOK PRODUCTION